Poetic Justice for the Soul...

Reflections of Poetic Expression

& Journal Entries for Girls!

Written By SistaKeeper Founder

Tracie Berry-McGhee M.Ed., LPC (Divine Tea)

Dedicated to the Cabanne Branch Library (My Keepers)

My mother, Margo, My daughters Khalia & Bria, my village and all girls developing a sense of self, finding their purpose to empower the universe! Never let society define your vision, your mission is to define you!

Know you're a Keeper!

Divine Tea

Table of Contents

Foreword (I am a Keeper)	5
I Define Me!	6
SistaKeeper Pledge	7
Free	8
This lil light of Mine	9
Hand me downs	10
Sallie	11
Enough	12
Soulfood	13
I Got GAME	14
I am Poetry	15
Keep Swimming	16
Harambee	17
Keepers vs. Cliques	18
I am Okay	19
Shoulda, Coulda Woulda	20
Mustard Seed Faith	21
Beautiful Flower	22
Role Model	23
Peace Street	24
Act like a Lady	25
Black Girls Rock!	26

Journal Entry Reflections (My Pledge to you)

I am who I am	28
I am unique	29
I am we	30
I represent Unity	31
I am Diversity	32
A mosaic of people live in me	33
I am my History	34
My Story is my legacy	35
My voice delivers solutions	36
My mind seeks knowledge	37
My spirit flows with purpose	38
I am inspired!	39
I am empowered!	40
I am naturally me!	41
I reflect positivity	42
I hold the key to my destiny	43
It's all about me	44
I define Me!	45
Tracie Berry-McGhee Bio	46

Forward

I am a Keeper! Poetic Justice for the Soul...

Reflections of Poetic Expression & Journal Entries for Girls!

Inspired by our Sistakeeper Circle Model Poetic Justice. Poetic Justice is an African-American Circle of Girls, ages 8-11 who participated in SistaKeeper for over ten years expressing their thoughts, fears, dreams and goals. The circles were held school-based as well as community based. This book can be offered to middle school girls as well.

The goal was that our girls realize their inner beauty early enough to not be threatened by societies views and they can realize that being a SistaKeeper means to above all be a SistaKeeper to yourself first, then seek your purpose to give back and be a Keeper to someone else. As girls and women we are Poetic Justice, empowered to build a positive sense of self, thus nurturing our personal mission and purpose in life to give back to our local, national and global communities.

As the facilitator the most common conversation was "I just want friends to accept me for who I am", "knowing that I am a Keeper and I define me!" This book of poetic expressions and journal entries captures thoughts and gives reflections to girls to share with each other, mothers with your daughters and mentors with your mentees. This is more than a book, journal and T-shirt that reflects positivity, this is a mission.

I Define Me! (Journal Entry)

My full name is…

My birthday is…

My favorite subject in school?

My favorite color?

My favorite food?

When I am alone, for fun I love to?

When I am with my friends, I love to?

My favorite singer/rapper?

My favorite song?

My favorite book/ movie or reality show?

My favorite line in my favorite movie?

When I dream of my future, I want to be?

I have many special gift/talents, I can?

When I define Me, I define me as?

I know I am a Keeper because?

Sign your Name

SistaKeeper Pledge

I am who I am, I am unique, I am We, I represent Unity!

I am diversity, A mosaic of people live in me, I am my history,

My story is my legacy

My voice delivers solutions, My mind seeks knowledge

My spirit flows with purpose!

I am inspired, I am empowered, I am naturally me!

I reflect positivity

I hold the key to my destiny

It's all about me!

I define Me!

I, _____

(Your name goes here)

Nurturing Inner Awareness

Knowing...

A SistaKeeper is You!

A SistaKeeper is Me!

A SistaKeeper is We!

S I S T A K E E P E R

Free

What does it mean to be *free*
The Sun,
moon,
stars, trees, flowers
and weeds.
Ocean, rivers, lakes, the seven seas...

Birds, Butterflies, lighthouses, GreenTea Sunsets and Rainbows
that bring you to your knees!
The meaning of you being you and me being me!

We must all find that happiness within to be able to just be!
Freedom comes from within, naturally.

Are you free to be who you want to be?
Rock to your own beat!
Never give up on living life!

Live your life to the fullest! Nurturing Inner awareness...
Being free means
I will accept you for you
&
You accept me for me!
Wherever I may be on my journey!
Free means to just BE...
What makes you feel free?

_____
_____
_____
_____
_____
_____
_____
_____
_____

This lil light of Mine!

This lil light of mine shine so bright touch the sky with all my might
Bring me stars to my room at night and follow my dreams wherever I take flight
This lil light of my mine, hold me tight and guide my feet through the darkest night.
This lil light of mine, never leave me!
Be my friend for life! This lil light of Mine.

How do you let your light shine?
_____
_____
_____
_____
_____
_____
_____
_____

Hand Me Downs

We all can use a hand me down to pick us up
A bag full of treasures, just for me! A book, a toy, a coat!
My favorite color, my favorite size,
they look brand-new in my eyes.

Shoes, skirts, dresses, and pants!
Old to you but new to me!

Hand-me-downs pick me up...ooh I really wanted it!
What was too short, too small,
Too big...became the perfect fit!
Thank you my Sista, I promise you I won't forget this!

Someone else's old becomes someone else's new
& it is just what we needed! Oh what a blessing!

Have you ever given your books, clothing, or toys away to bless someone else? If so, how does it make you feel?

_____
_____
_____
_____
_____
_____
_____
_____
_____
_____
_____

Sallie

Little Sallie Walker walks away in shame
No one wants to play with her they don't even know her name.
They talk about her behind her back and
won't let her play their games.

Little do they know if they only gave Sallie a chance
She would have been the best friend they ever had, but instead
Jack and Jill threw sticks and stones and shouted hurtful words
that made her hide and cry until she begin to seek self-worth
and Sallie grew strong enough to put herself back
together again.

Little Sallie Walker is a big girl now, leading others down the
right path and Little Red Riding Hood
And those Three Little Pigs have now become her best friends.

What does being a good friend mean to you?
_____
_____
_____
_____
_____
_____
_____
_____
_____

Enough

I love me enough to stand alone and not feel lonely

I love me enough to look at myself in the mirror and say please don't judge me

I love me enough to be a friend to me first when so called friends put me last

I love me enough to give myself second chances when I travel down the wrong path

I love me enough to be strong and try harder when enemies want to see me fail

I love me enough to be truthful to myself and have my own story to tell.

I Love Me…Enough

Write your own "I love me Enough" letter to yourself…

Dear _____

_____
_____
_____
_____
_____
_____
_____
_____
_____

Love, _____

Soul Food

I got rhythm down in my bones

I dance to the beat of the drum rolls

I got rhythm down in my bones

It was born in my soul, don't you know that my grandma's
Momma sang with Ella Fitzgerald when she was 54

I love jazz, rhythm & blues, gospel, hip hop and neo soul

from Mahalia Jackson to the Jackson 5

I've been singing since I was 5 years old

Yep, I got rhythm down in my bones

And it ain't got nothing to do with the

funky chicken or neck bones, I just know I got SOUL!

How does music make you feel?

_____
_____
_____
_____
_____
_____
_____
_____
_____

I got Game!

I'm not the average girl in your video

I got game!

Call me swish because I got it like that!

Call me touch because it's going down

Call me tennis because I make all the moves

Call me finish because I always make it to the line

I got skills like Serena & Venus, the WNBA,

like Olympic track star Jackie Joyner Kersee.

Like Nike, I just do it!

Like cows got milk I got this!

Now, I may not be built like a top model

but my athletic skills will make you wanna holler

because this girl right here is a baller!

Nope, I'm not the average girl in your video

But

I got game!

What sports do you love to play? _____

I am Poetry!

I write

I sing

I listen

I dance

I flow

I am poetry in motion

I lead

I follow

I whisper

I holla

I am the voice of tomorrow

I read

I write

I express my opinion

I define my destiny

I am Keeper of my Legacy

I am the future

I am Poetry!

Keep Swimming...

Are you a sista **N**urturing **I**nner **A**wareness through Poetry? Aah Snap!

Everybody needs a sista to reach out to another and set her free, yet we so deep into our own sea that we don't see the true meaning of

A SistaKeeper is You, A SistaKeeper is Me, A SistaKeeper is We!

Fear blocks us from reaching our destiny, child stop acting like a pretty little liar, or being a bad girl when you know you're Royalty!

Didn't Maya Angelou tell you "You are a Phenomenal Woman!"

Snap if you feelin Me!

You walk the halls looking each other up and down, like somebody stole your crown, you hate cause she rockin to her own beat, hatin cause her hair is tight, she smart, intelligent and trying to live right, so you start rumors and justify make-believe alibis when your confronted with your negative lies. Stop swimming in a sea of negativity! Ride the waves like a Real sista and say "still I rise!"

Remember, if she talked about the girl next to you, she will talk about you too. Hurt people, hurt people! Ain't that the truth! Ugly is ugly to the bone, so open up your closet and let that negativity go! It's time to reflect positivity! Tell the girl next to you, I define me!"

&

In the words of my friend Dory...

Keep Swimming! Keep Swimming! Keep Swimming!

Harambee

Kwanzaa makes me feel good, I give and receive and share food with my neighborhood, **U*jima*** *(cooperative economics)* collectively.

We are all smiles… no pain, anger, defeat, life's storms and rainy days. For these seven days we are here to celebrate!

I am blessed, renewed and rejuvenated!

Supporting businesses U*jamaa* **(Collective work)**, we renovating; buying everything under the sun!

Light the *Kinara (Candles)* as I set free my *Nia* ***(Purpose)***, today I am living and believing and having *Imani* **(faith)** knowing I am WE *Umoja* **(Unity)**, full of *Kuumba* (**Creativity**)screaming *Kujichagulia* **(self-determination)***!*

Holla if you hear me! Feel me! see me! Breathe… and let go!

As I scream in celebration seven times holding the last!

Harambeee!!! Harambee! Harambee! Harambee!

Harambee! Harambee! Harambeeeeeeeeeeee!

Keepers vs. Cliques

A clique is a group of girls who think they are the baddest chicks yet they spread negativity like it's the latest hit.

They participate in he say/ she say remixes but when you confront them they act like prefixes. They are wannabees who are trying to be Instagram famous while bullying other girls on Facebook and Setout pages.

Sista, remember being in a clique ain't cute unless your posing for a picture; know that in a insta- gram can slam your reputation quicker than that twitter! So stop acting like you're better than others, it doesn't make you more beautiful or realer; it makes you a straight hater or betta yet faker! Stop the snapchattin and know your better than that!

So stay away from the cliques and be a trendsetter, pick up your cell and say to your sisters I'm not following you! I am leader and being a positive Keeper is better than being in a negative clique on any given day.

Then KIK out, click your phone and walk away!

What would you say to a friend to stay away from negative cliques?

_____
_____
_____
_____
_____
_____
_____

I am OK

Missing pieces... who do you want to be? What do you want to do? Do you like to swim, dance, like to try anything new?

Do you want to be a teacher, a dancer, an engineer or an entrepreneur? Leader of the free world or the Queen of Egypt?

It's ok if you don't have all the answers; just know you have all the puzzle pieces, they are all inside and nothing is missing. You may not know all the small wonders of the world and the answers to the whys...

Just know that one day all of your "I don't know" and" I can't decide" will one day become "this is me and I've got to strive to be the best I can be and the one thing I do know is that GOD completely gave me all the pieces I need, I just got to seek them!

What do you know for sure about yourself?

_____
_____
_____
_____
_____
_____
_____
_____
_____
_____

Shoulda, woulda, coulda !

Never Say Never

Nothing beats a failure but a try

If you believe it you can achieve it

Your only competition is you

I can do all things through Christ

Never give up; give it all you got

Make it happen

Just do you

Define your shine!

Shoulda woulda coulda will never be an option in your vocabulary as long as you have try, and try again & try!

Make your own list of positive affirmations...

_____
_____
_____
_____
_____
_____
_____
_____
_____

Beautiful Flower

Beautiful flower growing tall reflecting the light of the Sun

I know that you don't know it all

but know that the seeds planted in you will make history someday

You are a keeper; keep your garden free of weeds, watering your needs daily. Feed yourself positivity and know that being a beautiful flower on the outside means nothing if it doesn't reflect your true inner beauty. Sow your seeds for the world to see that beauty grows naturally!

My beautiful flower!

What do you do to take of yourself inside and out (hygiene, meditate, exercise, etc...) or write what type of flower defines you? (sunflower, rose, daisy, etc)

_____
_____
_____
_____
_____
_____
_____
_____
_____
_____

Mustard Seeds

Soul food Sundays, fried chicken, turnip, collard greens, mac n cheese, gravy, Sunday school, pretty dresses & purses, handsome boys & praying circles.

Testimonies, bible scriptures, pastor preachin, Hallelujah!
Let the church say amen!

As granny slaps you in the back of the head and says "sit up straight, quit daydreamin, wipe your face, and put your money in the church plate" while the choir sings " Jesus is on the mainline tell him what you want!" and then she offers you a piece of peppermint candy.

As you leave church, the question is asked? What did you learn today?

And the answer is…

All I need is mustard seed faith.

What do you love and remember most about going to your church, mass, mosque, or synagogue?

_____
_____
_____
_____
_____
_____
_____

Who is your Role Model?

Who is your role model?

Take a look around you and tell me what do you see?
Do you see a beautiful person that reflects
who you want to be.

Who is your role model? Does she model positivity, loving herself, others and her community?

Is she your mother, teacher, sister or friend?

Is she caring, loving, creative, God fearing?
Does she challenge you to erase your fears? Empowers you to follow your dreams? Tell me who is your role model?

A role model is a keeper, a mentor, a person you know!
Not a singer, dancer or model from some reality show.

Sure those persons can display talents that you admire, but know that a real role model knows you personally and will be there when it really matters.

Tell me Who is your Role Model? And Why?

_____
_____
_____
_____
_____
_____
_____
_____

Peace Street... Blue Street has no more killings, no sexual abuse, just happy feelings. White Street is full of laughter, kids running free with no one chasing after them. On Black Street they can grow up and be who they want to be, full of power, families are growing and gardens have flowers.

Paintbrush in hand, I paint a land full of possibility! Were daddy's don't babysit, they are daddies and mommies don't just make cupcakes; they own the sweets and sale them.

Diversity Lane, and Character Court are streets full of poetry, and Love Street doesn't represent divorce but families that represent couples and families, straight and gay, full of hugs, affection, no prejudices, just unconditional acceptance. Love is simply Love!

Pink Street is breast cancer free, Red Street is strong full of life, HIV doesn't have immunity and Purple street is called "I define me" because it has self- worth. Domestic violence and suicide ended in the last century! Finally there are blocks and blocks of Hope Street, because being homeless is not reality.

On Peace Street we begin to pave roads to a journey were neighbors will watch neighbors and no one will ever have to stand their ground, because we are all keepers!
In our community, Peace Street represents Unity and is not a dream it's our reality!

What does "Being a Keeper" look like in your Neighborhood?_____
_____
_____
_____

Act like a Lady!

Good morning, please and thank you, yes sir and yes ma'am. Dresses and skirts just above the knee, clean bras and panties. Pantyhose and slips are bare necessities, so act like a lady!

Remember I taught you better than that, always remember somebody is watching, respect your elders, respect yourself, don't eat with your mouth open. Remember, girls are to be seen and not heard.

Never, ever sit on a man's lap, close your legs! Didn't your momma teach you better than that and if she didn't shame on her. You should know better, everybody knows that and if you don't then you do now, so act like it! Didn't she say do as I say not as I do even if she didn't practice what she preached? It's now up to you! It's okay you'll learn the hard way, besides you should know these things by now! You better straighten up and fly right, don't you know birds of a feather flock together! Don't let the doorknob hit you where the good lord split you.

You must think you're grown, get your hands off your imagination and No! You don't have nerves. I'm going to tell one more time, but you should know these things! Girl, you ain't grown yet! But you're as close as close can get! So act like it! Act like a lady!

What does it mean to act like a lady to you?

_____
_____
_____
_____
_____
_____

Black Girls Rocks!

Lights, Camera, Action

Look at me, I am a star!

A black girl who rocks! I'm going to go far!

Whether my hair is long or short, thick or thin.

Whether my skin is mocha chocolate or a hazelnut blend!

I am a descendent of my heritage and I know who I am!

I am a black girl who rocks!

My black is beautiful because of the way I talk and the way I walk. The way I play hopscotch and jump double-dutch!

I define my inner beauty and no one has to tell me I'm a cutie!

Lights! Camera! Action! No makeup can mask my true beauty

My mirror defines my true reflection not some random magazine or television station.

Lights! Camera! Action!

As I posed for the picture!

I am who I am, & I am a Black girl who ROCKS!

Take a picture of yourself or cut out positive words and glue it on this page!

Reflections of Divine Tea~Journal Entries

In the reflections of DivineTea, I wanted to inspire you through journal entries as well as poetry! I wanted you to know that poetry is my second love. My first love is my journal entries.

When I was in the 4th or 5th grade it started out simply writing to myself daily. I wrote all about how my day started and how it ended. I wrote about my friends, family and my deepest secrets, sealed with large letters of "DO NOT ENTER!"

I thought for the next few entries I would share journal entries with you. Written to you my little sisters; my advice to you to perhaps jumpstart you on your own writing journey.

The journal entries are titled by utilizing our SistaKeeper pledge as a theme for each journal entry.

I wanted you to know the meaning of each line. So when you recite it by memory you will own it and feel it in your spirit. As you read the journal entries feel free to begin to reflect and think about writing in your journal as well. Remember to OWN your NOW, this is your journey… Always be a Keeper to thyself first!

Nurturing Inner Awareness…

knowing

A SistaKeeper is U! A SistaKeeper is Me! A SistaKeeper is We!

I Am Who I Am

Dear little Sista,

I am writing to you today because I know it is difficult to look in the mirror daily and say "I am who I am" when you are changing every day. I really do understand, many times as I was growing up I would look in the mirror and my focus would be on my flaws or what I thought to be my flaws. I thought my lips were too big, or my hair was too short and I was too skinny. Seldom did I look at myself and feel I was beautiful.

So how about looking at it this way. Don't focus on the past or the future. Just focus on being the best you can be today. When you look yourself in the mirror just say out loud *I am who I am* and smile because after all on this day, in this moment no one can be you but you.

Remember look yourself in the mirror and simply say… *I am who I am.*

Your Keeper,

Divine Tea

I Am Unique

Dear little Sista,

How do you define unique? Unique can mean special, different, original… exclusive, or the one and only! Pretty cool definitions aren't they?

I like that unique means one and only because that tells me there is "only one" of you. No matter if you have sisters, brothers, or even if you are a twin. Who you are as an individual shows the world you are uniquely made. You have God and your parents to thank for that. You are an exclusive, (VIP) Very important person. So make sure that as you grow up you don't allow clothes or shoes to define you. Some people look for ways to label or judge you but you must remember you are uniquely made from the tiniest fiber in your hair to your big toe. Let the world know… *I am unique.*

Your Keeper,

Divine Tea

I am We

Dear Lil Sista,

When I was younger I didn't fully understand the concept of what "I am We!" really mean't until I actually went back to Africa to visit and saw our rich history. "I am We!" is an African proverb. In Africa it means we have a responsibility to each other. Our mothers and fathers, sisters, brothers and our community.

Therefore, if you are hurting then I hurt as well because you are my sista. If you succeed, I succeed, our community succeeds. Most importantly if you are happy then I am happy and the people around you see your happiness.

So remember when you see your people struggling have hope. Dealing with an illness or homelessness, or anything dealing with any type of negativity we must not look down on them. We must have hope.

We are all reflections of one another we must uplift each other every opportunity we get. Stay positive, pray and praise them because they are reflections of you and you of them. We are family and *"I am We!"*

Your Keeper,

Divine Tea

I Represent Unity

Dear Lil Sista,

Repeat after me "We are all in this together!" Unity means you and I represent togetherness. Together we stand, together we fall. Together we get back up and together we grow.

In today's society people always say to each other "I got me!" or I'm doing me! I'm Ms. Independent. Or I will take care of me, that is not unity!

Artist, Actress, Model, Rapper, Queen Latifah wrote a rap song called U-N-I-T-Y! It's beautiful to uplift each other. Listen to it when you get a chance. The Negro Nat'l Hymn Lift Ev'ry Voice and Sing makes me feel the same way! It gives you a spirit of unity! Of togetherness that you can take with you wherever you go.

Unity means we are a collective people with a rich history. Our ancestors were strong and represented a village of unity. They worked together, ate together and prayed together. We all carried with us the "I am we" inner voice that spoke outloud with dignity saying, *"I represent unity."*

Your Keeper,

Divine Tea

I am Diversity

Dear Lil Sista,

All of my ancestors life we have had to deal with prejudices and racism. Much of my life I have encountered it as well. It is safe to say you may experience it also. We have to find a way to counteract negativity. We can find various quotes from Nelson Mandela, Martin Luther King, Mother Teresa and the list goes on teaching us the importance of non-violence, acceptance and world peace.

"People all over the world, join hands on the love train, the love train." Such a cool song by a popular group called the Ojays. It makes me think of the best way to explain diversity. All types of people holding hands on a love train, embracing who we are. Unconditional love.

Diversity to me means we as African American girls live in a world of color. Within our race we embrace a sephora of browns, almonds, hazelnuts, peanut buster parfait, lemon, cantaloupe skinned sisters. Meaning we come in all shades of colors, light and dark; and different shapes. We are tall, short, thick and thin. Our personalities and family backgrounds have a lot to do with it. As you grow you will step out of your familiar space and meet others and you will see how we all have more in common than different. We must learn to be accepting of the differences whether we are respecting others religious beliefs, ethnic make-up, sexual preference or economic status. We are all created by the creator. No one can change that, but we can accept others for who they are. The key word here is, embrace. Our culture is the melting pot of diversity. We are a jambalaya of people from all over the world and that is what makes you and me know... *"I am diversity."*

Your Keeper,

Divine Tea

A Mosaic of People live in me

Dear Lil Sista,

Who are you? What is your story? When you know where you come from it is easy to respond. I am of African descent. I am from Europe. I come from Italy. I am come from Spain. Do you know???

My families history started in Mississippi and moved to Missouri. Regardless, of where you started we all have a rich history that goes back to the beginning. Just like art. Mosaic means we are pieces of art. Therefore, when you look at your culture you can embrace that we are all connected in a special way.

 God made sure that as we continue to grow as a people, checking off being black or white is not the only option. I am sure you have a rich history. Sit down with your mother, grandmother or grandfather and ask them to share where did your family come from. Don't you love family reunions when you get to meet family from different states and you can see we are from all over the world. We as a people can proudly say it loud I am black, I am proud, I birthed this earth! What can you say proudly about your heritage. I say… *"A mosaic of people live in me!"*

Your Keeper,

Divine Tea

I am my history

Dear Lil Sista,

Have you experienced your first family reunion or funeral? They can be a time of celebration and reflection. I was five years old when one of my grandmothers passed. Yep, I attended my first funeral before my first family reunion. I learned so much about her through my dad telling me stories and thank goodness for family reunions. During those reunions I would often meet the very people in the stories.

Family reunions and funerals; are the beginning of our lives and the end. Both occasions we come together and learn our history, meet family members, cousins, and distant relatives. These are the times when we must realize our past and our present have meaning. These are the times when we see patterns that we want to embrace and change so that our rich history continues or changes for the better. Our history is seldom taught in school, so the only way to learn is to seek it out and research yourself. You will be so proud of who you are.

In Africa, there is a saying called Sankofa. Sankofa means in order to know where you going you must know where you come from and you must always remember to look back and never forget. *I am my history.*

Your Keeper,

Divine Tea

My story is my legacy

Dear Lil Sista,

Do you know we all have a purpose, a reason to be on this earth? What is your story?

A part of the journey is that you tell the story of your life and it has meaning because it is after all… your story.

Legacy means what is left after you have passed on. Your legacy is a story that will be told over and over again about your beautiful life. My story is being written now, and I am happy to say, "so is yours." So make it worth it. As life unfolds let the world know of all the good things you have to offer.

When I first started dreaming and having goals I wrote it all down. I wanted the world to know I was a dreamer, a thinker and my thoughts turned into action and it didn't happen overnight. I bet you have a story to tell as well, let the world know…*My story is my legacy*.

Your Keeper,

Divine Tea

My voice delivers solutions

Dear Lil Sista,

This is one of my favorite parts of the pledge! It shows the world that you have a voice and you can choose to use it to deliver solutions, to make a statement.

Have you ever thought of screaming something outloud?

Say it loud… I'm black and I'm proud!

I want to make a difference!

I am a survivor!

I am who I am!

I define ME!

I am a Keeper!

When you speak up for yourself or your sista it is important that you promote positivity, compassion, courage and discipline. Action words that create change. Your tongue has power to hurt or to heal! Use your power! When you speak, stand up! Hold your head high, Be clear and say… *My voice delivers solutions.*

Your Keeper,

Divine Tea

My mind seeks Knowledge

Dear Lil Sista,

Please remember you are never too old to learn something new. I was once told knowledge is power and I believe it to be true. I was also told if you want to hide something from a black person, place it in a book. How unfair, but unfortunately literacy is not something many of us place at the top of our list.

My mommie loved to read, we both could read for hours! I felt when I was at home I had my own library. We even had a mini library in my grandmothers' house. When I was growing up the St. Louis Cabanne Branch Library was my safe haven; that is where all my knowledge began. I felt like it was my second home. The librarians even knew my name. They had a special area with all my favorite authors, like Maya Angelou, Nikki Giovanni, and Judy Blume.

My little sista, I demand that you always have a book in your hand! To ensure you are a well-rounded young girl, you must read, explore, and question anything you feel your mind is not understanding. Seek and you shall find. Always want to know. Read, visit the library, museums, and travel. Never be afraid to get on a bus, train or plane and just go. So when it was time for you to go to college you will be ready to grow!

My mother always had me in a dance class, acting, band, swimming, modeling, summer camps. I was always doing something to stimulate my mind to try new things.... Never be afraid to step out the box! The world is waiting! *My mind seeks knowledge.*

Your Keeper,

Divine Tea

My spirit flows with purpose

Dear Lil Sista,

Can you feel it? That tug in your stomach that says through God all things are possible. It is true. Everything you need is inside of you. You just need to tap into it, nurture it, and watch it grow into a sunflower. We all have many gifts and you were uniquely designed with purpose.

Remember the spirit inside of you is not something you have to think about! It sticks with you and you must learn to hear it, it is not loud or scary. It will always lead you in the right direction. It is your inner voice waiting for you to move with purpose on purpose. Sometimes you must be still, meditate and pray. I find it easier to allow my spirit to flow with purpose when I read the bible, just turn to wherever it opens, or read my favorite quote over and over again. Then I sit still and listen.

Dwell in it, connect your mind, and body. Walk in it and say… *My spirit flows with purpose.*

Your Keeper,

Divine Tea

I am Inspired

Dear Lil Sista,

I am inspired...because of you. All of the wonderful things you will accomplish in your life! We all must inspire each other through our dreams and desires. When I started journaling it was because I felt I had no one to listen to me, so when I would write I would inspire myself. What or who inspires you?

I challenge you as you continue to be a Keeper of your dreams to inspire yourself. Make a list of you goals, make a visionboard full of pictures of your future and be inspired to make it happen. Growing up in my neighborhood I never saw billboards representing positivity. Signs of inspirational messages and affirmations, but when I begin to explore poetry and magazines that reflected me, I began to be inspired! So my little sista seek positive images of yourself; first stop is your reflection. Continue to reach for your goals. I know you will reach each and every one of them if you remember to say to yourself, *"I am inspired!"*

Your Keeper,

Divine Tea

I am Empowered!

Dear Lil Sista,

I need you to listen to me, when you say to yourself "I am Empowered" those are strong words. "Em"- means we and "Power" means control. Therefore, as a SistaKeeper it means you must be empowered to be here for yourself and to be a keeper to your Sista. Now that does not mean fight her battles, do her homework or be her "Yes" girl. It means you will challenge either other, you will push each other to succeed, you will not stand on the sidelines when another sista is being bullied but you will find your voice and use it and empower her to use her voice as well!

Be empowered to find your purpose and change society and how it represents us in the media and in the world! Be empowered to to be a leader because you are dedicated to the mission, and the vision! Remember we can move mountains speaking out loud saying "I am Empowered!"

Your Keeper,

Divine Tea

I am Naturally Me

Dear Lil Sista,

When you think of being "naturally me" I want you to know it means more than wearing your hair in its natural state.

It means embracing who you are as a young woman. The natural girl that God made, not that society- made girl. Being natural is not a baby doll or a Barbie doll image. Being natural means we may have some flaws, may not be perfect yet accepting your imperfections as the aspects of whom we are that make us different.

Many young girls want to grow up and wear make- up, lipstick, change their hair from ponytails and braids to weaves and waves. That is okay, but we don't want you to change who you are because someone else thinks of you differently, or some magazine writes a message that speaks a language of not loving who God made.

When you look in the mirror, say to yourself "I like Me!" and if no one else does God does, that is all that matters.

Now, I know your saying DivineTea, the boys matter to me! I feel you! But anyone who doesn't accept you for just being you is not for you anyway. It's about loving you naturally inside and out.

So remember, you are wonderfully made in your natural state. No fake hair, fake nails, or fake personality can compare with a girl who says... *I am naturally me!*

Your Keeper,

Divine Tea

I Reflect Positivity

Dear Lil Sista,

How many times have you heard do as I say and not as I do? When I was growing up I heard it over and over again! What it mean't was even if our parents weren't doing what they asked of us to do, we still needed to do the right thing.

My question to you is, do you always do the right thing, even when no one is watching? Are you being a follower or a leader? IF someone is bullying a friend or a classmate do you say stop it, or model positive behavior. We must always be kind, and speak words that help others and not hurt their feelings. Maya Angelou one of my favorite poets once said "People may forget what you said, but they will never forget how you treat them" what I learned from that message is clear that whether I am looking in the mirror or hanging out with my friends I must always remember that… *I reflect positivity*.

Your Keeper,

DivineTea

I hold the key to my destiny

Dear Lil Sista,

In 2002, I sat down on a spiritual journey to ask God to direct my path. Pen in hand it was just the beginning of God's master plan. He was specific, the task was clear, my purpose was to impact lives through poetry. My calling was bigger than me.

Was I afraid? Yes! Terrified.

Did I say why me GOD? Yes! There are so many better writers out there. Then I realized the difference between when I am just writing and when I am writing with a purpose. It is like God is pouring out the words and later I say to myself "WOW! Did I write that?" I know then that I am just a vessel.

Trust me little sista I am not a perfect person, but the gift that God has given me… you can't put a price on it! I had to trust knowing I had what it took, the faith of a mustard seed. So I began to write and write and write. Double doors began to open and I heard messages clearly. So now I repeat to myself daily (and so should you)… *I hold the key to my destiny.*

Your Keeper,

Divine Tea

It's all about me!

Dear Lil Sista,

"It's all about me!" to some people can sound quite selfish or have a negative tone. So I knew I must take the time to break this down. So many times in your life you will see people putting others before themselves, their goals, aspirations and even dreams.

You must remember to look in the mirror and not allow others to dictate what you see. When you're struggling with weight issues, color barriers, or decisions that will impact your life forever remember you must block out negativity. Find a cheerleader, be your own or find someone on your side that believes in your vision.

Yes it is all about you! You are fulfilling God's purpose in your life. Others need to see the true meaning of I respect myself, I love myself, and I honor myself. Of course you know it is bigger than you but for you to stay on the path you must be able to so stand alone and say yes… *it's all about me!*

Your Keeper,

Divine Tea

I Define Me

Dear Lil Sista,

I define me was an affirmation we started saying in 2003. My daughter had become very aware of labels that society would give others. People can be rude and opinionated. Some people may say out loud or think to themselves look at her, or you're different, weird, strange, and peculiar.

Some people would even have the nerve to judge people because they are short, or tall, because a person was diagnosed with ADHD or has physical disabilities or limitations. The worse was if you had a life threatening illness. We are even judged when we announce to the world we have cancer, lupus, sickle cell or HIV. Stereotypes and bias toward others is plain ignorant. The only solution is awareness.

My daughter began to say to the world, stop judging me! Labels don't define me! Not the labels, clothes, or your judgmental words. So we began to wear t-shirts, lanyards & wristbands that promote self- awareness and letting the world know that you define your shine and you're a keeper to yourself and to others as well. Who are they to judge? You must decide that you will not allow others to point fingers and define your direction because you know the meaning of being a Keeper, knowing…
I define me!

Your Keeper,

Divine Tea

A SistaKeeper is you!

A SistaKeeper is me!

A SistaKeeper is We!

A SistaKeeper is you

A Sistakeeper is me!

A SistaKeeper is We!

A SistaKeeper is you!

A SistaKeeper is me!

A SistaKeeper is We!

S i s t a K e e p e r

TO My SistaKeepers...

Universally, Sister is spelled with an (er) meaning biological sisters. SistaKeeper spells "Sista" with an (a) because we are **All** a sista, women of color, therefore all girls can benefit from this toolkit because we all represent the rainbow of diversity. If you open up your multi-cultural crayola box and find your color, SistaKeeper is for you! It's Just-US! Poetically we define we!

I am a Keeper... is a part of the Imani Project, a stepping out on faith mission, sent to me on my healing journey. To be able to reach out to my sisters of color, remembering I must know who I am, know my history and never forget to reach back and pull another sista forward to make a difference. I must be aware that I am a Keeper!

My purpose is to empower my Sista. My obligation is to heal the next generation through poetry, therapy, journaling and motivational speaking. Healing the next generation is every woman's responsibility. In order to be of any value collectively, we must learn to heal ourselves first. A SistaKeeper does just that! It helps you to heal yourself! So explore, listen, reflect, journal and meditate. Then take the steps to put into action what your mission is and make a difference.

If you're a interested in being a Keeper, it is simple take the pledge, promote the mission through wearing our Nia Tees (T-shirts with a positive message promoting HIV Awareness, Breast Cancer Awareness, Domestic Violence Awareness and Self-Awareness) Most importantly seek your purpose to being a Keeper to yourself first!

Poetically Speaking... Divine Tea

Tracie Berry-McGhee, M.Ed., LPC, Author, Therapist, Entrepreneur, Speaker

Tracie Berry-McGhee M.Ed., LPC poetically speaking (DivineTea), a native of St. Louis, MO. received her Bachelor of Arts in Psychology in 1990 and her M. Ed in counseling, in 1998 from the University of Missouri, St. Louis.

She has written and produced a spoken-word CD, and self-published The Red Book (for teen girls) SistaKeeper Poetry for the Soul , I am A Keeper, and a SistaKeeper Curriculum and journal designed for African-American girls seeking to find self, and become aware of their purpose. In 2004, SistaKeeper Empowerment Center became a nonprofit organization in St. Louis, MO and now has presence in Africa, Jamaica, New Mexico and Germany. The goal is nurturing inner awareness, building self-esteem, developing purpose in girls and women. Her goal is to feel stadiums with girls nurturing empowerment.

Today, her purpose has led her to establishing the Nia Group STL, a wellness center for women where she currently provides prevention, intervention and awareness through individual counseling, facilitating mentoring circles through SistaKeeper and promoting young women finding their purpose through motivational speaking engagements in local, national, and global communities. Her goal is to travel the world inspiring girls to find their voice, defining their self-worth and nurturing their purpose.

As a dynamic speaker, therapist, and consultant through her continuous commitment Tracie Berry-McGhee, has demonstrated her dedication to diversity and the empowerment of young women today. She is a member of Delta Sigma Theta Sorority Inc., Saint Louis Metropolitan Alumnae Chapter, and a member of Christ the King, UCC. Tracie is the wife of Nathaniel McGhee, proud mother of three beautiful children Khalia, Bria, and Nathaniel. Most importantly she is a child of GOD!

For booking information visit

www.niagroupstl.com

www.tracieberrymcghee.com

When God tells you to walk run like the wind for you are guaranteed to fly~DivineTea

This is my testimony, so with faith(Imani) as my obsession I ran, ran pass my fears, pass pain, and right into the arms of Purpose (Nia)!

Nurturing Inner Awareness in girls to be a Keeper to thyself and others!

I am now forever renewed and set free to be the woman that God purposed for me to be, sowing seeds in my sisters locally, nationally and globally. I am your forever Soulflower Sista...

Your SistaKeeper,

Poetically Speaking...DivineTea

Nurturing Inner Awareness...

SistaKeeper Mission & Vision

Vision

SistaKeeper empowers young women to be inspired to develop their mind, body & spirit into women with a strong sense of self and purpose, dedicated to making a difference in the lives of themselves, and their community.

Mission

SistaKeeper creates a society of young women who know who they are, what they believe in, and what they stand for. They can make educated choices, be assertive, display teamwork and be true to self, fighting for issues that plague our communities, thus, becoming cycle breakers.

This "I'm a Keeper!"

Journal Belongs to

_____

My SistaKeepers

This journal is all about you!

Be inspired, be empowered, be a Keeper to your dreams, create your destiny! Say the SistaKeeper pledge to yourself daily! Be a Keeper!

Share your thoughts, feelings, poetic expressions and journal entries as you begin to nurture your spirit, to recognize the power and strength within, allowing you to search for the answers and proceed to make a change. Educate your mind, reflect and nurture your spirit, celebrating individuality. Allow the pages to manifests purpose by empowering you to develop the authentic self within to make a difference.

Peace Within,

Tracie Berry-McGhee, M.Ed., LPC

Poetically Speaking… Divine Tea

I'm a Keeper!

I'm a Keeper!

I'm a Keeper!

I'm a Keeper!

I'm a Keeper!

I'm a Keeper!

I'm a Keeper!

I'm a Keeper!

I'm a Keeper!

I'm a Keeper!

I'm a Keeper!

I'm a Keeper!

I'm a Keeper!

I'm a Keeper!

I'm a Keeper!

I'm a Keeper!

I'm a Keeper!

I'm a Keeper!

I'm a Keeper!

I'm a Keeper!

I'm a Keeper!

I'm a Keeper!

I'm a Keeper!

I'm a Keeper!

I'm a Keeper!

I'm a Keeper!

I'm a Keeper!

I'm a Keeper!

I'm a Keeper!

I'm a Keeper!

I'm a Keeper!

I'm a Keeper!

I'm a Keeper!

I'm a Keeper!

I'm a Keeper!

I'm a Keeper!

I'm a Keeper!

I'm a Keeper!

I'm a Keeper!

I'm a Keeper!

I'm a Keeper!

I'm a Keeper!

I'm a Keeper!

I'm a Keeper!

I'm a Keeper!

I'm a Keeper!

I'm a Keeper!

I'm a Keeper!

I'm a Keeper!

I'm a Keeper!

I'm a Keeper!

Made in the USA
Middletown, DE
03 November 2024